T0129462

THE ROAD TRIP

*RV Misadventures
on a Budget*

M.L. ROBERTS

authorHOUSE®

AuthorHouse™
1663 Liberty Drive
Bloomington, IN 47403
www.authorhouse.com
Phone: 1 (800) 839-8640

Published by AuthorHouse   11/05/2018

ISBN: 978-1-5462-6647-1 (sc)
ISBN: 978-1-5462-6678-5 (e)

Library of Congress Control Number: 2018913012

Print information available on the last page.

ACKNOWLEDGMENTS

Thanks to my family and friends for the inspiration. Without them, this story would have never come to fruition.

CHAPTER ONE

The Bargain Buy

I'm not a prissy person, honestly. I'm down-to-earth but not one who likes roughing it either. I'm a frugal, middle-aged, petite blonde lady who watches every cent our family spends. However, when a reasonable opportunity for adventure is available, I'm ready to go and will look for the most affordable option. So, when the opportunity to "invest" in a preowned motorhome came at a reasonable price, my husband, Brad, and I jumped at the chance to own a vacation home on wheels.

For our upcoming summer vacation, my husband, Brad, and I decided to purchase a cheap, used motorhome that we hoped would only require a couple of minor cosmetic repairs. We wanted to find a fully enclosed unit so that we would have the freedom to move around inside, forage for snacks from the refrigerator, use the bathroom as needed while on the road, and be surrounded by the comforts of home. The only problem was that we were uncertain about getting locked into a monthly payment for a luxury item, and we only had six thousand dollars in cash. I relentlessly searched RV websites, "for sale by owner" listings, and other online advertisements.

Eventually, I found a great bargain online for a motor home listed by a private owner located in Orlando. This was less than two hours' drive time from our hometown of Brandon, Florida. The listing described a motorhome in good condition and fully operational for only fifty-five hundred dollars or best offer. It sounded like just what we were looking for and was within our price range. Brad contacted the nice gentleman, and we headed out to Orlando for what we hoped was a good deal.

The motorhome was a thirty-three-foot Class A model, Pace Arrow, fully enclosed, with two large windshields up front and narrow windows along each side. Although it was twenty-five years old, it seemed to be in considerably good condition, with only cosmetic issues such as fading beige exterior paint and peeling pinstriping on the sides. The odometer indicated only thirty-six thousand miles on the motor, and the gentleman stated it was mostly highway miles. He told us that the motorhome was taking up too much space in his small yard, and since his girls had grown up and moved out, he and his wife didn't need something so big to travel in. The motorhome filled the entire width of his driveway and expanded lengthwise from the garage door to the curbside near the adjacent street. It seemed quite obvious that he had good reasons to want to sell.

As soon as I stepped up through the side entrance to the interior, I was greeted with decorative aesthetics that could only be called retro. I felt like I had been transported back to the late seventies. Shag carpet in various shades of brown spread throughout the motorhome, even in the closet and bathroom. The window treatments encrusted the sides of the glass windows with frail brown velour, faded and aged from years of sun exposure. Some of the speckled white paneling revealed coffeelike stains, which the gentleman stated as minor water damage. But what else should we expect from a bargain buy?

The kitchen had a small double sink located below a sliding window, a propane oven and stove, a compact overhead microwave, and a refrigerator with a minuscule freezer. Inside storage was substantial, with cabinets running lengthwise across the top of the ceiling on the driver's side, where pots, pans, and dishes could be stored. There were also lower kitchen drawers alongside the oven for knives, forks, and other utensils. On the passenger side, cabinets spanned from behind the upper bunk bed along the ceiling to the side entrance door. Underneath those cabinets and situated behind the passenger seat, two cushioned bench seats faced each other, with a small dining table in between. On the other side of the entrance door, a long wood-paneled closet stretched along the wall to the shower unit. The closet had three mirrored doors and an interior hanging rod for clothes. Underneath the closet, four pull-out drawers were available in which three pairs of shoes could possibly fit in each.

The shower unit itself was barely large enough to fit one person of average body size and was colored dark mustard yellow. The shower had a screen enclosure in the ceiling and a window crank to open the skylight roof vent. The stall door was made of flimsy plexiglass, framed in tarnished gold-colored trim. Across the two-foot hall from the shower, there was a narrow closet door, and inside it contained the toilet and a bathroom sink with a cabinet. The small room could put a claustrophobic person like me on edge with the door shut. Thank goodness it had a small sliding window for air circulation and miniblinds for privacy.

The sleeping arrangements allowed for five people to snooze comfortably. The entire back bedroom and bathroom area could be sectioned off with an accordion divider for privacy. This area had two separate twin beds, each one lengthwise on the sides, with a two-drawer wooden bed table separating them in the middle. There were cabinets above and below each twin bed for more storage. Underneath the passenger-side bed, the fresh-water tank took up half the storage space. The space under the driver's-side bed opened up to the exterior storage access. Up front, behind the driver's seat, the sofa folded out into a double bed for two people to sleep comfortably in close proximity to each other. A drop-down plastic bunk bed with a twin-size mattress ran along the width of the motorhome, above both the driver and passenger captain seats. When the bunk bed was not in use, it could be pushed up into the ceiling and fastened closed with two plastic clasps.

Another fine amenity was air conditioning throughout. There were two units, one in the back area by the bathroom and the other in the front kitchen section. However, only the front unit was working when the owner demonstrated the operation of this fine rolling home to us. The one unit proved to cool the entire living quarters easily. With all these conveniences at such a bargain, we excitedly purchased the Pace Arrow motorhome and planned our family vacation.

CHAPTER TWO

Maiden Voyage

Our first family excursion in our new-to-us pleasure cruiser was to be a weeklong camping expedition to a fishing lodge and campground in the Lower Florida Keys. Sean, a coworker from the security company where Brad worked, told him about the lodge and campground. He enticed Brad with exciting stories of hunting spiny lobsters in the Keys during the season opening in August. We figured we would give it a try and attempt to catch ourselves some "bugs," as they are known. Since we lived in the Tampa Bay area, the drive to the Lower Keys would take just over six hours with our Sea-Doo jet boat in tow.

Brad and I had visited the Keys on previous vacations with our kids, Kevin and Kelly, and stayed in hotel accommodations while on the islands. On those trips, we would enjoy the snorkeling excursions, such as the Dry Tortugas exploration and the Christ of the Abyss adventure located in Key Largo. However, Kelly and Kevin had never experienced hunting for spiny lobsters, and now a twenty-four-year-old Kevin was stationed in Germany, serving in the army.

At the time of our trip, Kelly had blossomed into a beautiful twenty-year-old with fair skin and long, dark-brown hair, the same color as her father's hair. I lovingly called her our Snow White princess. We now also had a bright blue-eyed, blonde-haired, two-year-old daughter, Cindy, our little Cinderella. My becoming pregnant with Cindy at forty years of age came as an absolute surprise for the entire family. I guess that is what happens when your husband spends most of the marriage on night shift and then switches to day shift. We definitely spent more quality time together after the shift change.

Brad's mother, Marge, had never been to the Keys either. Lobstering would be a new experience for the three of them. Since Marge resides in Oklahoma, she flew into Tampa just for this summer vacation adventure with all of us. Marge is a no-nonsense spunky little sixty-seven-year-old blonde-haired lady who stands less than five feet tall. When mad, she reminds me of a fussy Chihuahua, but she truly has the kind heart of baby kitten and will go to great lengths to help anyone.

Upon Marge's arrival, we packed the motorhome with all the basic necessities such as dinnerware, clothes, toys, fishing gear, snorkeling accessories, and groceries. Brad hooked the Sea-Doo trailer to the motorhome hitch and confirmed the brake lights worked on the trailer while I pumped the brakes. Our plan was to head south to the Keys with me following behind the motorhome in my car, a silver Suzuki Verona sedan. I was driving the car separately, just in case we wanted to do some sightseeing in the Keys without having to drive the mammoth motorhome around. Cindy and Kelly were both glad to ride in the comfort of the motor home, leaving me all by myself for the long, lonely ride in the car.

Most of the drive was along Interstate 75 heading south. Since my front scenery was the tail end of the motorhome and boat, I entertained myself with playing music CDs and finding whatever pop stations were available on the radio without static. When we started traveling through the section of interstate called Alligator Alley, I strained to see as far as I could through the fence line for any alligators popping their heads out of the water, but without success.

Before we got to the bridge heading over to the Keys from the mainland, Brad pulled over at a gas station, and I followed him in. He parked alongside a gas pump and began filling up the motorhome. I parked on the other side of the pump and filled up my car also. At fifty dollars, the gas pump stopped on him. For the motorhome, that would only be half a tank of gas. Brad swiped his debit card again, and it was declined.

After a couple of swipes, he yelled over to me in frustration, "Mickie, come try your debit card on this stupid thing."

I had already completed filling my tank, so I walked over and swiped my card. It was declined too.

"Huh? I just used it. Well crud, I bet the bank just put a stop on our cards. I'll call the bank and let them know it's us."

I pulled out a credit card and swiped it so he could continue to fill up the tank with gas.

While sitting in my car waiting for Brad to get situated and back on the road, I called the bank. After going through the automated voice service and verifying my personal information, a live person finally answered the phone line.

"Yes, Ms. Roberts, how can I help you today," the polite customer service lady inquired.

"We're unable to use our debit cards. Can you check on the problem, please?" I replied.

"It looks like a hold was placed on your debit cards due to unusual transactions occurring. Can you please verify the transactions?"

"Well that explains the issue," I thought. "Yes, ma'am," I replied.

"We're showing two gas purchases at the A-1 Truck Stop in Florida City."

"That's us," I said cutting her short. "We're driving a large motorhome and my car separate. It costs quite a bit to fill the tank on the motorhome. Please make sure our cards are activated. Our credit cards will be used too."

"Thank you, ma'am. Whenever you are traveling, please make sure you set a travel notice for the unusual transactions."

"I definitely will. Thank you."

As I finished talking to her, I started the car and followed Brad back out onto the main road. I was quite impressed by the security protection from the bank but would've been highly ticked if we couldn't use our debit cards all week.

As we drove south down US-1 through Marathon Key toward the Lower Keys, Marge called me on my cellphone. She urgently hollered, "Brad says the motorhome is running hot. He's going to pull over at the next gas station."

"I'll follow him in," I replied and thought, "Oh no, this really can't be good."

Brad pulled over into a convenience store, and I pulled in after him. Steam poured out from under the hood as he lifted up the metal cover and braced it with the inside rod. He discovered the water lines on the radiator had come loose. The radiator was bone dry with no water. Frustrated and sweating from standing in the ninety degree summer heat, Brad and I went into the store to find out if they had a water hose which we could use to refill the radiator with water.

Now I hate to be stereotypical, but wouldn't you know that the store clerk was a gentleman of India decent who spoke broken English. Brad kindly asked him, "Do you have an outside water hose? Our motorhome overheated, and we need to put water in the radiator."

In his broken English, the store clerk flatly said, "No hose."

"You got to be kidding?" Brad muttered under his breath as we walked toward the back of the store out of the clerk's earshot. "Here's our plan," he tells me. "We buy two one-gallon bottles of water from the store and fill them up from the bathroom over there," he said pointing to the door with the Women's restroom sign.

As planned, I bought two one-gallon bottles of water and walked them outside to Brad. I started making repeated trips in and out of the store, filling the gallon bottles from the Women's bathroom sink. Obviously, I was in a foul mood and dared the store clerk with a glaring stare to say something to me.

Brad finally clamped the water lines back together and the radiator was filled to the brim with water. The motorhome fired right up, and we were back on the road to the Lower Keys.

Upon arriving at the Fly-Fishing Lodge and Campground, Brad passed up the entrance of the drive for the campground and boat ramp. The road dead-ended into the end of a canal so there was no possibility to drive around the block. He had to maneuver the motorhome and boat trailer through a tight u-turn without ending up in the mangroves located on either side of the road. I stood roadside directing him around like an air traffic controller and could hear him cussing while trying to steer. I just prayed Cindy wouldn't pick up on his foul language.

When Brad finally got the motorhome turned around and pulled alongside the lodge entrance, I went into the reservation office and paid for the campsite and boat slip. The desk clerk provided me with the lock combination and site map.

Once she completed the transaction and gave me the paperwork, I walked back outside and approached the motorhome.

"How are you planning to get the boat in the water?" I asked him through the driver's side window.

"I'm going to back it in with the camper, how else?"

I groaned, visualizing a sinking motorhome in my head as Brad started driving it toward the boat ramp. Our friend, Sean, ran up to me.

"What is he trying to do?" he asked, shaking his head in doubt. "There ain't no way he's gonna back down that ramp and see what he is doing. He's gonna sink the boat or the camper."

Sean left me and ran over to the driver side window while yelling at Brad, "Hey, hey, let me back it in with my truck."

"Naw, I got this. Just let me know when it's in the water," Brad replied stubbornly and continued to back the trailer down the ramp and into the canal.

I walked back to my car praying and shaking my head in disbelief. From my driver's seat, I continued to watch him make multiple attempts trying to align the motorhome and trailer on the ramp, cussing and fussing with each attempt.

He eventually maneuvered the trailer straight into the canal, and I breathed a sigh of relief when he stopped and hopped out of the motorhome to push the boat off the trailer into the water. After stepping up on the trailer frame, he balanced precariously while stretching to wrap the tie-rope around the boat cleat. He pushed the Sea Doo boat into the water and then climbed back up and off the trailer frame while holding the tie-rope end. He pulled the boat over to the canal wall with the rope and fastened it to the available cleats.

After making sure the boat was secured, Brad ran back to the motorhome and drove it and the trailer off of the boat ramp and parked the trailer on other side of the canal.

I started my car and drove up to the lodge entrance gate which was a thick chain fastened with a combination lock. In order to open the lock, I had enter the combination the number provided by the desk clerk. After finally figuring out the lock, opening the chain gate, and driving through, I parked on the side of the drive and waited for Brad to follow.

Once he drove through with the motorhome, I walked back over and locked the chain back together.

Since Brad didn't have a clue where to go, I pulled the car out in front of him and started the drive past the lodge toward the campground sites.

The lodge itself is a two-story coral-colored bungalow style building with mint green shutters on each of the windows. The front of the lodge facing the main street houses the reservations office and a store full of necessities such as refrigerated goods like milk, eggs, and cheese. For the avid fisherman, the store sells fishing equipment such as fishing line, hooks, and grotesque frozen dead fish for bait. The store also provides Florida Keys souvenirs for tourists such as t-shirts, coconut-shaped citronella candles, flip-flop shoes, and my favorite, key lime salt water taffy.

The side section of the lodge houses some of the hotel rooms which face the boat ramp on the canal. The guests can dock their boats in the slips in front of the rooms for ease of access for lobster and fishing excursions. Along the backside of the lodge, there is a dance hall and a drink bar for evening parties. Across from the dance hall, a game room is setup for kids and adults to play arcade games, shoot pool, and play table tennis.

On the upper deck of the lodge, there are more hotel rooms and an outdoor swimming pool with lounge chairs and tables placed around the outskirts of the concrete deck. A tiki hut with another drink bar is located at the pool entrance.

As I drove past the lodge toward the campsite, I noticed a small separate building with a sign "Laundry Mat." I smiled to myself, satisfied that I had loaded up on quarters and packed a bottle of laundry detergent for the week. As I turned the corner, I noticed the playground with a lonely slide and a swing set with empty swings bouncing in the breeze.

"Cindy will probably have fun over there," I thought as I continued to follow the path toward the campsite.

Since the start of lobster season is a big event in the Keys, several campsites were already occupied with motorhomes of different lengths, styles, and brand names. Many of owners were bustling around their campsites setting up their chairs, tables, outdoor lights, and canopies to create the effect of home away from home.

As I circled around the outer bank of the camping area, I noticed the primitive tent city section with the colorful nylon structures bobbing playfully in the sea breeze. I thanked my lucky stars that we would at least have the comforts of home in the motorhome instead of roughing it in a tent like those along the outer bank.

I continued down the path to the canal campsites and counted the site numbers based on the map provided to me from the desk clerk. Brad followed me closely from behind. When I pulled up alongside the campsite, I abruptly stopped the car and hoped he would manage to stop quickly too. I hopped out, and yelled at everyone in the motorhome, "We're here!"

CHAPTER THREE

Margarita Misery

Our campsite was situated beside the canal with water and electric hookups and a well-worn wooden picnic table. Brad eased the motorhome into the campsite slot with help from Marge and me in guiding him into the tight space. As soon as he stopped and turned off the engine, the girls came bouncing out of the motorhome full of energy from being cooped up so long from the road trip. Cindy couldn't wait to get her bathing suit on to go swimming with Grandma Marge and Kelly in the big upstairs pool that she had heard so much about from our friends.

As the girls and Marge walked off to the pool area, Brad left to retrieve the boat from the ramp to dock it alongside the campsite in the canal. Since I was left by myself, I figured it was time to enjoy some peace and quiet and a frothy cold drink.

I dug the blender out of the overhead cabinet, pulled the drink mix and tequila from the fridge, unloaded ice from the freezer, and chummed myself a heavenly frozen margarita. I dragged out a reclining chair from the outside storage cabinet and stretched out, sipping my delightful concoction while soaking in the sun on my face and body.

After a few minutes, I heard the SeaDoo engine and heard Brad whistle. "Well, so much for peace and quiet," I grumbled under my breath.

I walked over to the concrete wall where he pulled the boat in alongside. He tossed me the rope and hung out the boat bumpers as I pulled the boat and him up closer to the wall. As I bent over and wrapped the rope around the wall cleat, I felt a little light headed and thought, "Yep, that was a good margarita."

Later in the afternoon, Brad and I headed over to the lodge pool with the kids and grandma. Our friends, Sean and Mary, and other guests were swimming in the pool, lounging on the poolside chairs, or hanging out at the tiki bar while enjoying drinks and chicken wings.

Brad ordered some mango rum drinks for him, Marge, and me, sodas for the girls, and a stack of the chicken wings for all of us to munch on for dinner. The mango drinks were deliciously sweet, and I loaded up on them without even realizing how many I had to drink while I chatted and mingled with new friends in the pool. I was feeling good and giggly, enjoying the ocean breezes, and nothing could bring my spirits down.

In the evening, Marge, Kelly and a sleepy Cindy walked back to the motorhome, and Brad and I visited with friends at the picnic table outside their room beside the canal. We played games of quarters and drank shots of Jaegermeister and Red Bull. My head eventually started spinning, and Brad had to carry me back to the motorhome, not that I remembered him doing that exactly. I had overextended my drinking escapade and had managed to get toasted drunk on the first night in the Lower Keys.

In the morning, I paid miserably for my first night of frolicking. I woke to find myself spread out on one of the back twin beds, hugging the pillow to my head. My brain throbbed and pounded like it was going to explode from a tight shell. I lugged myself out of the bed and dug in my purse for aspirin, knowing it probably would not touch the pain. The throbbing pain in my head made my stomach wretch, and I staggered quickly to the toilet and vomited unrelentingly. I prayed for mercy with my face hanging in the plastic toilet.

From the front of the motorhome, I overheard Marge ask Brad if the kids weren't drying themselves off good enough from swimming because the carpet was soaking wet by the bathroom door.

I felt the motorhome sway side-to-side as someone walked through the front section. In my condition, every movement and sound brought me nausea, and I again started puking from the motion.

Brad opened the back section divider and stepped into the bed area where I had crawled back into one of the beds and was balled up in pain.

"How you doing puky?" he inquired with a smirk on his face.

"Just peachy, or should I say mangoee? I'm swearing off alcohol the rest of the week," I replied pulling the pillow back over my pounding head.

Peeking out from under the pillow, I watched as he stepped around on the wet carpet area, tapping it with his toes, with a frown on his face. He bent down and pulled back the carpet from around the bathroom door and groaned. "The waterline's dry-rotted. It's cracked and leaking."

He lifted up the twin bed mattress across from me where the fresh water tank was and shook his head, "The water's coming in from the fresh water tank ... well crap. We're not going to be able to use the water anymore."

Water had leaked along the floor, and his only option was to cutoff the water from the outside hookup to the motorhome. This made the shower and sinks unusable. That was the last thing I wanted to hear with my pounding head and upset stomach.

Even with my brain in pain, I came up with an idea so I could use the toilet for my vomiting episodes. Thank goodness we still had the two one-gallon water jugs from the convenient store! I pulled the gallon jugs out of the closet and dragged myself out to the water spigot by the motorhome to fill them full of water. As I puked my brains out all day in the toilet, I used the water from the jugs to flush my mess down the toilet hole. I crawled back into the bed, miserable and mad at myself for making a mess of our vacation.

As I held the pillow over my head in the back bed of the motorhome, I heard Brad and Kelly talking by the canal about going lobstering. I heard the boat start up and then there was still silence. Eventually, I fell into a much needed deep sleep and did not wake up until the next morning. I lost over a day's vacation in the Keys from a massive margarita mango rum Jaegermeister hangover. Never again!

During my hangover escapade, Marge proved to be a blessing as always. She took care of little Cindy when I couldn't even take care of myself. Marge entertained Cindy with swimming in the lodge pool and playing on the swings on the playground. She even put up with me yelling at her to turn down the ringer on her phone because of my splitting headache. I could only handle hearing the ringtone, "The Devil Went Down to Georgia," when I was sober. And, in the spirit of the great outdoors, Marge hand-washed our dirty dishes by the campsite water spigot.

Our water fiasco also restricted us to using the campground bathroom facilities for showers. This proved challenging since vicious biting noseeum bugs swarmed the campground around dusk. These awful critters fit their names quite well. We could not see them until we were already bitten. The only life-saving products were Deep Woods Off insect repellent or Avon's Skin So Soft. Otherwise, we had to be fully clothed and sweaty in the warm evening temperatures. So much for taking a shower between sweat and repellent …

CHAPTER FOUR

The Pain of the Hunt

When I finally got my marbles back together for hunting lobsters, we planned a day for us to all go out on the jet boat. In the morning, Brad made omelets and bacon in frying pans on the table-top grill while we sat around the picnic table. An older gentleman camper, Chuck, walked up and started chatting with Marge. Chuck's probably in his seventies and spent several years vacationing at the lodge. As he stood there talking incessantly to Marge, Brad offered Chuck a lawn chair to sit in.

"Here Chuck, have a seat. Would you like some eggs?" Brad asked.

"No, I'm good. Thank you," he said as he sat telling Marge about lobstering and how long his family had been coming to the lodge for vacations.

"Well, I better get," Chuck said as he started get up from the chair. As he pushed himself up, the left arm and leg broke off the lawn chair, sending the elderly Chuck plummeting backwards onto the ground. He sat there dazed for a moment, and Brad ran over and helped him up.

"Sorry, about that Chuck," Brad apologized. "That chair came with the camper. I had no idea it was in bad shape. You okay?"

"Yeah, yeah," Chuck said brushing the sand off. "I'll be fine. Nothing I can't handle. Ya'll have a good day and good luck with the lobsters."

As he waved and walked off, Brad said, "Man, I feel bad about him and the chair. I had no idea how rickety it was. I pulled it out of the camper storage. It must've rotted from sitting in there."

Marge sat snickering, "Well, I guess you cured him of coming around here flirting with your mom, didn't you, Son?"

That he did. We didn't see much of Chuck after the chair incident.

After finishing up breakfast, we headed out on the boat and jetted along the outskirts of No Name Key which is located just east of Big Pine Key. Marge and Brad took turns dragging Kelly and me behind the boat on ski ropes while we wore masks and snorkels in search of spiny lobsters. The ocean water was crystal clear and a greenish shade of blue. Small colorful fish darted in and out of coral fans and barrel sponges as we floated across the ocean floor. It was like flying over an underwater desert with the corals and sea life resembling cacti and desert plants. The underwater scenery was breathtaking.

When Kelly and I did see a spiny lobster, the chase proved to be challenging for us. We both have buoyant bodies. By the time we would find a lobster and dive down for it, we were out of breath and would have to resurface to make another attempt. Brad finally figured us women were useless together as lobster hunters. He jumped into the water to snorkel with me, leaving Marge, Kelly, and Cindy on the boat to watch anxiously for signs of lobster.

As we floated around in the water, a spiny lobster nonchalantly walked under Brad, like it could care less about us being there. It must have been watching Kelly and me earlier and figured it had nothing to worry about. Brad dove down after the lobster, attempting to slam a handheld net over its body in order to trap it. The lobster shot back toward me. My reflexes kicked in, and I slammed my legs together, catching the lobster between my thighs. OUCH!! There's a reason they're called spiny lobsters. The spikes across the sides of its body poked into my flesh. I was in pain but held tight. Brad swam behind me with the net and tapped me on the back to let me know to release my thighs. I let go relieved. Bingo!! We finally caught a spiny lobster!

After crawling back into the boat, I looked down and saw I had pinhole markings on my inner thighs where I had held tight. Marge stared at me, "What happened to you?"

"I caught a lobster!" I replied with a smug smile.

"It looks like you hugged a porcupine with your thighs," she laughed.

"Whatever works to get the job done," I said rubbing my thighs for some relief and to try to remove the pinhole indentions.

After a few more attempts by Brad, in which he successfully caught a couple of more lobsters, we headed back to the lodge. Brad showed Kelly and me how to pop the heads off the bodies and use the antennas to clean the "poop" out of the lobsters. We were both pretty grossed out and agreed he could do the lobster cleaning. Kelly and I decided we would help with the hunting and eating, and eating is exactly what we did. Grilled lobsters with garlic and butter are delicious, and that's exactly what we had for dinner.

The next day, Brad and I attempted our luck again for lobsters, and the girls decided to stay back with Grandma Marge at the pool. It was a long, unsuccessful day. The water was cloudy and visibility was poor underwater, which made spotting the lobsters even more difficult. As we headed back around the island to go in, we heard a siren. A Florida Fish and Wildlife officer pulled up to the boat.

"Ma'am, I need to check your boat to see how many spiny lobsters you've caught," he said sternly.

I looked at him in absolute frustration and responded by holding up my thumb and pointer finger in a big fat zero shape. "We have nada, not even one. Come on aboard if you want. There's nothing here."

My face must have told the whole story, and my truthful frustration prompted him to respond, "Never mind. I think you're good," as he backed his boat away.

Brad smiled as he started back toward the channel, "Guess he figured you were having a bad enough day, he wasn't going to mess with you. You scared him, you mean woman."

"Yeah, whatever. I'm tired and hungry. We can take a break and go back out later in the afternoon with Kelly."

I should have stopped while I was ahead and empty-handed. After eating some lunch and taking a short nap, we headed back out on the boat with Kelly. Brad drove the boat while pulling me along on the ski rope with Kelly keeping a watch over me. Suddenly, a film hit my mask, and I felt burning across my chest and upper-arms. I let go of the rope, yelling "Come get me!" I felt like I was on fire.

Brad circled the boat back around, and I crawled up the back ladder and flopped myself onto the boat cushion. My chest and arms had red welts across them, and they were stinging like I had swum through a bees' nest.

"Oh my god, I'm on fire! What hit me?" I asked while drenching my chest with fresh water from a drinking bottle.

Kelly looked over the side of the boat and said, "Mom, I know what hit you. There's jellyfish everywhere."

I looked over the side. Sure enough, there was a swarm of jellyfish around the sides of the boat. They were big and gelatinous with a cloverleaf-like design on the top. I strained to remember what I had read about jellyfish stings. I vaguely recalled that using vinegar could help to remove the stingers and alleviate the pain caused by the venom.

"Please get me back to the lodge. I need to get some white vinegar on me. I'm hurting."

Brad turned the boat toward the island, and we flew at top speed until we reach the no wake zone. As soon as I reached the canal wall by the motorhome, I darted into the motorhome and found my wallet and ran non-stop to the lodge store. I quickly found the white vinegar on the food shelf and was bouncing up and down waiting for the desk clerk to ring it up. She looked at me funny and then smiled. "You must've gotten stung, huh?" she inquired.

I thought to myself, "Duh, the marks on my chest were a giveaway." Instead I nicely replied, "I sure did and need to take care of the stings now. Keep the change."

I grabbed the bottle and ran back to the motorhome, found a washcloth, and dabbed the white vinegar on the marks across my chest. At first the vinegar stung, but within a few minutes, the pain subsided and became a little more bearable.

Brad and Kelly came inside to check on me. "How are you doing, Mom?" Kelly asked.

"I'm okay. The stinging is going away. Whew, I'm glad you weren't in the water or you would've been stung too."

"No kidding, thank goodness," she replied.

After sitting at the picnic table and relaxing, I decided to call it quits for the evening and went to the bathhouse to take a shower and douche my stings again. When I returned, Marge and Cindy were back from the swimming pool and getting ready to hit the bathhouse too. At that point of our trip, I had enough of lobster hunting to last me a while.

Our total catch of spiny lobsters for the entire week was only eight legal-sized "bugs." It was a pathetic count in comparison to our friends who in total bagged more than two hundred spiny lobsters. Guess it helps when you have a few well-bodied young men who can hold their breaths a long time when diving. Brad was now obsessed for us to become certified divers before our next lobster trip, so we could stay underwater longer. I also decided I was getting me a wetsuit as protection against jellyfish.

CHAPTER FIVE

Farewell to Paradise

At the end of the week, we packed up and headed back northwards home to Brandon. As Brad drove the motorhome along the bridge from Big Pine Key to Marathon, I followed him in close proximity. While jamming to the music of The Who's song, "Pinball Wizard," I noticed a black object shoot out from the driver side wheel of the boat trailer. It jumped across two lanes of traffic, and a truck in the oncoming lane swerved to miss being hit by it.

The wheel on the trailer started gyrating unsteadily. "Oh crap," I thought to myself and immediately tried calling Marge on her cellphone. No answer. That was to be expected since I remembered I asked her to kill the volume of her Charlie Daniel's ringtone when I had my hangover.

Next, I tried calling Kelly in a panic. She answered smoothly, "Hellooo."

In a frenzied voice I yelled, "Tell your Dad to pull off the road immediately when he gets off the bridge. He's about to lose the driver side trailer wheel!"

"Oh, okay," she replied. I heard her in the background repeating my message to pull over. Then she replied, "He said he would."

As soon as the bridge ended into regular roadway, Brad continued driving. I'm thinking, "What is this stubborn fool doing?"

He finally pulled off the road into the parking lot for a trailer repair shop and walked out to take a look at the trailer wheel. I had pulled in behind him and jumped out of my car.

"What happened?" I asked.

Brad bent over, inspecting the tire, and grimaced, "The wheel bearing and cap are missing. I'll check and see if they have replacements here." Brad walked up to the trailer repair shop. The office manager said he couldn't help. Instead, he redirected us to another trailer repair shop a couple of blocks down the road.

Brad climbed back into the motorhome and drove slowly with me following close behind with my hazard lights flashing. As soon as we pulled into the next trailer repair shop, an elderly, thin and worn looking man walked out of the shop. Brad showed him the problem with the wheel bearing, and he said, "No problem. Ya'll go getcha some lunch, and I'll have this repaired in no time."

We piled into my car and drove to the nearest restaurant just a block down the road. After filling up on burgers and fries, we headed back to the trailer shop. The boat trailer sat there repaired and ready to go. The elderly man had replaced the wheel bearings on each tire. He said, "Noticed the other wheel was getting ready to do the same thing, so

I went ahead and replaced it too. I didn't want ya'll to get stranded since you had that grandbaby with you."

I busted out laughing looking over at Cindy, who stood there oblivious while intently picking at the rubber on a tire. "Grandbaby? I hope you're going by Brad's looks and not mine. That's our baby girl!"

One of the other shop guys came up and rescued the man from embarrassment by saying, "No ma'am, he was talking about you, little girl. You look like a grandbaby."

"Yeah right, good try," I replied sarcastically. "How much do we owe you?"

"One-ninety for both."

I gave him two hundred cash and told him to keep the ten as tip for rescuing us.

We headed back out on the road driving northward on Alligator Alley. I kept an ever watchful eye on the boat trailer and the motorhome instead of alligator hunting this time. We finally made it back home with no more problems.

CHAPTER SIX

On the Road Again …

Once home, Brad replaced the water lines with new pvc pipes and installed a secondary radiator fan to help keep the motor cool. He said he thoroughly checked the motorhome for any other issues. We had made plans to work our jobs the next week and then take another road trip the following week to transport Marge back to her homestead in Oklahoma. While en route, we planned to do a scenic tour of the Southeastern states and do some sightseeing.

As planned, Marge and I busily packed up the motorhome on the Sunday morning of the following week. We gave Kelly hugs and kisses goodbye. Kelly had to start back to college that week and reluctantly could not go with us on the trip to Oklahoma.

From our last experience in the Keys, I remembered this time to log into the bank's website and set the travel notices for our debit and credit cards. I had a feeling we would be buying a lot of gas on this excursion and did not want problems in being declined.

On our way up through north Florida, we stopped in Ocala where Brad's sister, Jeanie, and her husband, Darnell, lived. During our brief visit, we joined them for dinner at a local sports bar. It was already after seven o'clock in the evening when we finished eating, so we decided to camp out in their front yard overnight. Since they lived out in the country on five acres, they had plenty of available space for us to park the motorhome. The stay provided Marge with an opportunity to enjoy some quality time and beers with her daughter, and Cindy was able to spend some time with her aunt and uncle. Her Uncle Darnell gave her an oversized SpongeBob pillow for the trip.

As the time pushed past nine o'clock, exhaustion overtook me and Cindy became whiny and cranky. I tucked her into one of the twin beds with SpongeBob, and she immediately passed out. I told everyone goodnight and stretched out on the opposite twin bed. Later, I heard Marge and Brad come into the motorhome. Brad slept on the bunk bed, and Marge stretched out on the couch.

Brad woke us up the next morning at five o'clock before sunrise. He couldn't sleep and was anxious to get on the road. It started misting rain outside as he guided the behemoth through the gate and down the dirt street winding past Jeanie and Darnell's house. Cindy stayed fast asleep and did not budge even with the bouncy movement of the motorhome over the bumpy road. I figured I would try to get more sleep so that I could take over the driving duties later. But sleep was not going to happen for me. Even the asphalt roads were bumpy, and I felt like human popcorn kernel being bounced around the back of the moving motorhome.

Eventually, I gave up on getting anymore sleep between the bouncing and the call of nature for the bathroom. Luckily, I didn't have to attempt balancing myself in the miniature closet bathroom because Brad spotted a fast food joint and his belly called to it for breakfast. Cindy had also awakened and was ready to eat. Brad parked toward the backside of the parking lot and ran inside to get our orders. Cindy and I split a big breakfast with pancakes, sausage, and hash browns while Brad drove and munched on his bagel and egg sandwich. Marge was glad to have some coffee and an egg sandwich to help kick her into gear too.

After we ate, Cindy played with her building blocks on the floor for a few minutes. I stretched out on the couch, figuring I should try again to get a nap so I could take over the driving duties. Cindy inevitably crawled on top of me and fell back sound asleep. I was getting sleepy myself but my arm was cramping from Cindy laying on it. As soon as I almost dozed off, Brad asked, "Do you want to drive?"

Again, I figured I might as well get up since sleep wasn't going to happen for me. I asked him, "Where are we?"

He replied, "We're in Plantation, Georgia," as he pulled the motorhome alongside the gas pumps at the convenience store.

After filling up the motorhome with gas, he asked me again, "Do you want to drive?" I reluctantly groaned.

Marge piped up, "Come on now. You got to drive and prove to your mom and yourself that you can do this." Marge was egging me on because my mom had made the statement in front of her that I had problems driving my dad's "home-made" motorhome when I was an inexperienced teenage driver. She knew that reminding me of the comments would make me want to prove myself.

I've always pushed myself and tried to follow my dad's saying of "Can't never could do nothing. If you think you can't, you won't."

If I wasn't so tired I would be ready for the challenge. Instead, I groaned again and reluctantly crawled in behind the steering wheel. "Where's everything at on this contraption?" I questioned Brad.

Brad pointed out the light switches, the wiper controls, how to use the cruise control, and how to pivot the steering wheel.

"Just remember, this ain't your car. You have thirty-three feet that you need to make sure you get cleared of anyone else on the road," he instructed.

"I know, Brad. I'll make sure I'm clear."

I started the beast up and headed toward the northbound entranceway onto interstate I-75 North. As soon as I merged into the right-hand lane, the driver side door swung open. I grabbed at it quick and slammed it shut while trying to steer with my other hand. I yelled at Brad, "Thanks for shutting the door!"

He said, "Well, I came back through the other side door." Now I was at least fully awake from the adrenaline rush of panic due to the door opening.

As we headed through Georgia toward Atlanta, Marge and I gossiped about other family members and the incidents we've had with them. She loved antagonizing me with pointing out restaurant signs and asking me if I was hungry yet. She knew I would get annoyed since I had told her that when traveling with my mom, it seemed like she was always wondering when we were going to stop and eat again. Marge would teasingly yell, "There's a Cracker Barrel! When are we gonna eat? I'm hungry."

I glared at her while giggling said, "Look old lady, you can get off your butt and get something out of the fridge. There's ham, cheese, and bread. You'll have to hold the mayo and mustard since we forgot to pack any." We both cracked up laughing.

As we started getting closer to Atlanta, a rush of eagerness surged through me to prove my driving abilities. My confidence had increased within the short amount of time I had been driving the motorhome. I told Marge, "I just have to drive the interstate through downtown Atlanta. Mom would never believe I drove this humongous motorhome through this crazy interstate system."

I whipped the motorhome along the narrow lanes and in what seemed to be in close proximity to other cars. I kept a watchful eye on the portable GPS navigation system, read my handwritten directions, and maneuvered the steering all at the same time. Marge pointed to one of the green interstate signs and said, "You need this exit."

"No, that'll send us east toward Savannah. I need to stay in this lane for I-20 West toward Birmingham, Alabama. You really do want to go sightseeing don't ya?"

"I'll keep my mouth shut. You know what you're doing better than me," she conceded. "I'm impressed you can navigate and drive too. I've driven many times with a map on the steering wheel while driving myself places too."

CHAPTER SEVEN

The Blow-out

By the time we maneuvered through Atlanta, it was later in the afternoon, and we all were all starving again. I was unusually hungry thanks to Marge pointing out all the restaurant signs to antagonize me. Brad had awakened refreshed from his catnap and asked, "Where you want to eat?"

"How about us get out of this tuna can and get something decent?" I asked. "Geez, I'm starting to sound like my mother," I thought.

Around that time, I had seen the blue interstate "Food" sign designating the restaurants for the upcoming exit. A steakhouse restaurant was one of the selections on the sign and seemed to suit my taste buds and hunger just right. I clicked on the right-turn blinker and slowly pulled off the exit.

The steakhouse was located in front of a strip mall, and the parking lot was full closer to the restaurant building. In order to be able to park the monstrosity, I would have to find two empty adjacent parking spots.

I headed toward the end of the lot where there were less cars and more empty spots available. A Chevy sport utility vehicle was parked on the right side and a Cadillac was parked on the left side of the two vacant adjacent spots. It was going to take some maneuvering and patience, which I felt like I was starting to run short on thanks to driving through the tight lanes in the parking lot.

Brad crawled up and sat behind me on the sofa since Marge was in the passenger seat. He piped up again repeating, "Make sure you swing out far to get the rear end around. You know you got thirty-three feet to pull clear. It's not like parking your car."

"Yeah, yeah, I know. Quit telling me that! I'm trying." I said, annoyed and stressed at this point. I steered wide to the left to get the rear end of the motorhome around.

Brad yelled, "Stop, stop you're gonna hit the other cars! You want me to park it?"

"Yeah, I might be able to drive it, but I obviously suck at parking."

I shifted into park, slid out of the captain seat, and walked to the back end. I peeked out of the passenger side window over the bed. We were less than three inches away from hitting the Chevy.

"Oh crap!" I yelled to Brad. "You'd better watch the passenger side. It's really close to the SUV."

He carefully backed out of the spot by checking both the rearview mirrors and was able to reposition the motorhome midway in the adjacent parking spots without hitting either of the vehicles. It was nerve racking to say the least.

Even with a full parking lot, there was no waiting time for being seated at the steakhouse. The hostess immediately directed us back into the dining area. Although I was extremely hungry, I wanted to watch what I ate. Even with being nauseated and hung-over in the Keys, I had managed to gain five pounds and didn't want to put on any more weight from this trip. I figured whatever I ordered, I could split with Cindy. I ordered a cheeseburger with french fries. Real healthy, I know. Brad ordered himself a sirloin steak with steamed broccoli to share with Cindy too, and Marge asked for a bowl of French onion soup.

After a hefty lunch, we loaded ourselves back into the motorhome with Brad at the wheel. After about an hour of driving, Marge said her stomach wasn't feeling well and asked Brad to stop at a convenient store when he could. He asked her, "Why do I need to stop? There's a toilet onboard so use it. I fixed the water already. I just don't want to be dumping the tank all the time from us using it."

Marge disappeared into the closet bathroom and came out saying she felt better. About thirty minutes later and before arriving in Birmingham, Alabama, a late-model black Camaro pulled up beside us. The well-dressed man inside the Camaro honked his horn erratically and frantically pointed toward the back of the motorhome. He pulled in front of us and turned on his right indicator signal while waving toward the emergency lane. He then pulled into the outer lane with the intentions of us stopping behind him. Brad turned on the hazard signals and stopped behind the Camaro. The man hopped out of the car and ran toward us.

I said, "I wonder what he wants."

"Well if he wants to rob us he won't get much," replied Marge.

Brad rolled down the driver side window. The man had to yell over the interstate traffic. "You lost this huge black tank with hoses sticking out of it a few miles back."

Brad asked him, "Is there anything still hanging down under the motorhome?"

The man looked back at the rear of the motorhome and replied, "There's a grey tank hanging down, and it looks like it's getting ready to fall off too."

Brad told him thanks, and the man ran back in his car and took off. I asked Brad, "Are we going to go back and get the black tank?"

"Oh, hell no!" he laughed. "The cops would probably be looking for a motorhome without a septic tank. Can you imagine the damage it could've caused? I am going to pull off at this exit and see what happened."

He turned off onto the interstate exit and pulled into a gas station parking lot alongside the gas pumps. We all got out and looked at the back of the motorhome. Sure enough, the grey holding tank was dangling from the underneath straps. Brad said, "Well, I'll be damned. Frankie and I had checked those straps before we had left for the trip. Guess they were in worse condition than I had originally thought."

I exclaimed, "Frankie helped you?" Now granted, I adore my cousin and he tries hard, but he has the worst luck it seems like when he works on stuff. Go figure that since he touched the motorhome, something would fall apart.

As Brad started working on pulling the grey holding tank out from underneath, a straggly, skinny black man carrying a brown paper bag staggered up to him. He asked Brad, "Where ya'll from?"

"Florida," Brad replied annoyed.

"Really? I always wanted to go to Florida."

"Well I always wanted to leave," Brad responded in a sarcastic manner while yanking on the tank.

"I'd help ya out if you'd give me $1.50 to get a beer to complete my six-pack."

Brad was past aggravation at this point and grumbled, "Can't help you. I don't carry cash." The man staggered on without saying another word.

While Brad dealt with the tank situation, Cindy and I went inside so I could pay for the gas in advance. The pumps were old-fashioned and without credit card readers. And again, I hate to stereotype people, but sure enough, the cashier was of Indian descent. I told him "$100 on pump three, please."

"You need $100 in gas?" he questioned, staring at me with an unbelieving look.

"Yeah, look at the monstrosity we're driving."

"Oh, okay. Where you from?"

"Florida."

"You going to Florida?"

"No. We're heading to Oklahoma from Florida."

"Well you then you have safe trip," he said nicely as he finished processing the receipt.

Cindy and I walked back to where Marge and Brad were standing at the back of the motorhome. The grey holding tank was now sitting on the ground, and it reeked with the smell of stagnated water.

"Oh yuck, what are you planning to do with that?" I asked Brad. "It stinks. Please tell me you're not planning to put it inside, are you?"

"Well, he thought about strapping it to the top of the roof," Marge replied.

I looked bug-eyed over at my mother-in-law. "I can see us going through a tunnel or under a bridge, and it getting ripped off and hitting a car. That's really not a good idea."

Brad walked around to the storage cubbyhole located on the driver-side at the back of the motorhome. He shifted some things around and shoved the tank into it. The tank fit with no problem, and luckily the stench did not ooze into the inside of the motorhome.

After we climbed back into the motorhome and settled in for the drive, we started cracking jokes at Marge. "Damn, I knew old lady poop was bad, but I didn't think it'd blow off the septic tank!" Brad laughed. "What'd you eat?"

"All I had was French onion soup and some sweet tea," Marge snickered. "I guess my stomach really did hurt to do that kind of damage."

"Well, I guess we can still use the toilet to pee in. Just don't take a crap. You'll see the road through the opening in the bottom of the toilet. If you take a crap, someone behind us is going to get it on their windshield," Brad joked.

"Gross. Guess it would be a good way to get rid of tailgaters," I chuckled.

CHAPTER EIGHT

The Long and Bumpy Road

As we kidded around about our toilet fiasco, Brad drove west along I-20 with Hot Springs, Arkansas, as our intended destination. When we arrived on the outskirts of Birmingham, Alabama, the highway road became extremely bumpy causing everything inside the motorhome to shake and rattle. Once in a while, a screw would fly out from somewhere and hit me as I sat in the passenger captain chair. I would add it to the collection of screws growing in the console change tray.

The bumps in the road eventually became too much for the motorhome to bear, and the bunk bed plastic clasp above the driver side snapped loose and fell off. Marge and I fought with trying to hold up the bed on the driver side and popping the plastic clasp back on. As we fought with it, Brad hit another bump, and the passenger side unclasped and the entire bunk bed dropped down, almost hitting him on the head while driving. As he drove scrunched down in the seat driving, Marge and I frantically tried getting the entire bunk bed pushed back up and clasped closed while being bounced all over the floor. Brad started yelling, "You got to do something with it quick, or it's gonna drop on me. I can't drive like this!"

"We're trying. I can't hold it and get it clasped too!" I yelled over the rattling. "Find a place to pull over!"

My arms started to hurt as I continued holding the bunk bed up while waiting on Marge to get the clasps back in place.

Next thing I know, Marge busts out laughing. It was contagious. I started giggling too.

"Stop it! You're making me giggle, and I'm going to drop it on his head," I snickered at Marge.

"I can't help it. I think I'm going to pee myself laughing," Marge giggled and snorted.

I was finally able to compose myself and push the bed back up. Marge clamped the driver side clasp back on, and I closed up the passenger side. "Thank goodness," I sighed with relief as I fell back into the passenger seat.

Brad looked up over his head and slid back up into his seat. "Keep an eye on those clasps just in case they come loose again."

Sure enough, the clasps took turns popping loose during the rest of the day. Even Cindy would point and yell in her toddler babble, "Ed, ed," for "Bed, bed." Marge or I would immediately pop the clasps back down so the bed wouldn't drop on Brad's head. When the asphalt road became smoother, the clasps stopped popping, and we forgot all about the problems we were having with them.

Since it was starting to get dusk, we decided to look for a campground. The GPS directed us to the Millworks

State Park in McCalla, Alabama. After pulling in and making reservations, we discovered that the park had several camping sites, a public park with a crystal clear creek, a large playground, small convenient store, and most importantly, immaculate bathroom facilities.

As soon as we got the motorhome parked and situated at the campsite, Brad and I decided to walk Cindy over to the playground to let her release some pent-up energy. As we walked the paths, we noticed the campground was practically full, and several children were out riding bicycles while others were playing along the side of the small creek. Cindy stopped on the wooden footbridge that crossed the creek and watched the other children playing in water. She pointed to them, indicating she wanted to play too.

"No honey, we're going to take you to the playground to go swing and go 'weee'." I told her, making a swinging motion with my hand. She bent over and picked up a pebble and threw it into the water. That must have been enough to satisfy her curiosity because she turned and started heading toward the direction of the playground.

The campground convenient store was located along the path to the playground, so we stopped in and picked up a couple of drinks to quench our thirsts. I bought a cold can of grape soda and enjoyed sipping it as we walked. When we arrived at the swing set, I sat the soda down on the bench by Brad while I pushed Cindy on the swing.

After letting Cindy spend some time on the slides and playset, we got ready to walk back to the campsite. I went back to the bench and picked up the can to take a sip of grape soda. A yellow jacket-like bug flew out of the can opening. I screamed, "Oh crap!" in the middle of the playground and threw down the can, startled by thinking I could have been stung.

Other parents in the area glared at me with evil-eyes that said, "How dare you use such language in front of my child!" I was extremely embarrassed and felt like crawling into a hole. I already had enough excitement for one day and was ready to call it a night.

When we arrived back at the campsite, Marge was busying herself with making grilled ham and cheese sandwiches for dinner. After munching on the sandwiches and eating some potato chips, I asked Brad if we could use the shower. "No, you can't use the shower. The water will run underneath the camper, and it will be too obvious. We're going to have to use the bathhouse."

"Dang it," I replied and packed up the bathing soap, towels and clothes for Cindy and me. I tromped off over to the bathhouse with my toddler in tow.

The next morning, we all woke up early and ready to go. I was hoping we would make it to Hot Springs that day. I had never been there before and was curious to see what the city was like. As I hopped in the passenger captain chair, I said in a bubbly voice, "Lord, what do you have in store for us today?"

I think the Lord's response was "Ask and ye shall receive," by the events that happened next.

CHAPTER NINE

Never a Dull Moment

After having breakfast at a Waffle House, we drove into Tuscaloosa on I-359 and then picked up state road 82 heading west. As we started moving along the bumpy road, I quietly realized to myself that we never resolved the problem with the bunk bed. And, since I was paying more attention to the bunk bed then where Brad was driving, he missed the exit for 82 and had to backtrack northeast.

Suddenly the motorhome hit a divot in the road, and the bunk bed busted loose again, almost hitting Brad in the head. He ducked in the neck of time. I pushed it back up and clasped it close again with Marge's help. Marge conjured an idea. "If we have a clothes hanger or wire, we can wire the clasp together around the screws to hold the driver side up. That should keep it shut and stop the other side from popping loose."

She pulled out Brad's toolbox from the closet and started digging through it for a pair of pliers.

"There's a clothes hanger in the closet. I'll get it. Just watch the bed to make sure it doesn't come down again," I told Marge.

Of course, Brad hit another bump, and the bed came slamming down again.

"You got to do something with it!" Brad hollered, scrunched down in the seat.

"That's it! You have to pull over or exit. I can't hold it and fix it. I don't know why you didn't fix it last night!" I yelled back in frustration.

Brad finally pulled off an exit into a gas station parking lot. Marge had started modifying the clothes hanger into a wire to hold the broken clasp together. When Brad stopped and parked, he helped push up the passenger side of the bunk bed into its clasp. Then he finished modifying the clothes hanger to hold the both driver and passenger side clasps closed.

"That should hold it," Marge said.

"I think I'm pulling that bed out of here when we get back home. That thing's dangerous." Brad said shaking his head.

I could only agree, especially since my arms were starting to hurt from the several times I had held the stupid thing up.

After making certain both the clasps were tightly secured, Brad pulled the motorhome over to the gas pumps and filled up the tank. He climbed back in and asked, "Everyone ready to go?"

"Yep, as much as we can be," I replied. He directed the motorhome back toward the entrance for state road 82 and started heading west again. We drove for a little while and enjoyed the peacefulness of the countryside scenery. Marge sat on the floor with Cindy, playing with the building blocks. I was in the passenger seat and looked up over at Brad when the motorhome home started chugging and making sounds like it was attempting to stall. It sounded like it was running out of gas.

"You're playing around, right?" I asked, hopeful that he was just pulling a trick on me.

"No, that's not me," Brad replied.

He was coming upon on a gas station on the right, and I said, "Pull in there." He ignored me and kept going.

I thought, "You've got to be kidding" and slumped down into the seat.

The motorhome finally stalled, and Brad coasted it along a woodsy roadside with tall grass and no buildings in sight.

"It's gotta be the fuel pump," he groaned. "But I just replaced it before we went to the Keys."

"And, you couldn't have stopped at the gas station?" I asked in a sarcastic tone.

I immediately placed a call to road assistance from my cellphone while Brad and Marge went outside. Brad crawled underneath the rear of the motorhome and pulled off the electric fuel pump. Marge stood back smoking a cigarette in the tall, dry grass. I looked out at her and thought, "Yep, good way to catch us on fire … geez woman."

After getting up off the ground, Brad sat down on the entrance step and opened the fuel pump. The electronics were fried and the inside of the pump was pitch black and smelled of burnt electric wiring.

The road assistance operator finally answered, and I tried telling her where we were located. I hadn't been paying that much attention after Brad had reached state road 82 heading west. By what I could figure, we were somewhere between Tuscaloosa and Gordo.

The female agent listened to my attempt at directions and replied, "We'll send a tow truck driver out there to you."

"The problem is that we're in a motorhome and just need a fuel pump. If they could bring it to us or if they could drive my husband to a parts store that would really help us out," I said in a panicked voice.

"Oh," she responded intently, "Let me transfer you to the service company for that area." I heard music and then dead air. I had been disconnected.

While I had been on my cellphone, Marge had made more progress on her cellphone finding a parts dealer in the area. There was a parts store just 3 miles away according to the GPS. Brad was at the point of walking to wherever he needed to go to get the fuel pump.

Marge handed him the cellphone to talk to the parts salesperson. He told the man, "I'm stuck here off of 82 westbound with my family. If you could help us out, I'd really appreciate it."

The man offered to bring a couple of different Chevy fuel pumps, hoses, and clamps right to our location. Brad told him, "Thank you so much. I really appreciate your help."

When the man showed up, neither of the fuel pumps were correct. The man and Brad climbed into the truck and headed out to the parts store. While they were gone, Marge sat back on the sofa drinking a soda and Cindy and I played with her alphabet barn on the dining table. The red toy barn had cutouts for plastic-formed letters A, B, C, and D to be dropped into from the top and four animals with different shapes to match along the front of the barn. I held up the letter "A" and asked Cindy, "Where does this letter go into?"

She sweetly replied in her toddler voice, "In the A-hole!"

Marge choked on her soda and gasped, "What did she just say?"

"It goes in the A-hole, Meemaw," I giggled. "Out of the mouth of babes. The B goes in B-hole, C in C-hole, so the A goes in the A-hole."

"Oh my gosh, it sounds so funny with her saying it," Marge chuckled.

Not too much later, Brad and the parts salesman returned back to the motorhome with the correct fuel pump. Brad tried giving him a $20 tip for his trouble.

He said kindly, "No, sir. I didn't mind helping you and your family. Just if you ever see me in a restaurant, buy me a glass of tea."

Brad thanked him again and crawled back under the motorhome to install the new fuel pump.

Marge stood outside again watching Brad wiggle around under the back end of the motorhome while smoking another cigarette. I was getting antsy and needed to go the bathroom. I poked my head out the door and whispered to Marge, "I have to go pee. Where's Brad at?"

"Oh, he's nowhere near the septic hole. You'll be okay. Go ahead," she replied as she waved at me to go on.

I went inside the closet bathroom with my bladder feeling like it was going to burst. What a relief! I pushed the pedals at the bottom of the toilet and stepped out the bathroom doorway.

Brad yelled, "Mickie!"

Marge busted out laughing and hacking at the same time. Sure enough, I had wet Brad down with my pee and potable water. The water had run across the underneath of the motorhome frame and had sprinkled on top of him.

"I had to go, and she said it was okay!" I pointed accusingly at Marge while laughing my butt off.

"Just consider it payback for anytime you felt he crapped on you," Marge snickered.

I know I must have a wonderful mother in-law when she lets me pee on her own son. He must have definitely given her a hard time growing up.

I still felt bad for poor Brad. He went ahead and finished hooking up the fuel pump and then came inside and took a quick shower to get my mishap washed off of him. Of course, all the water ran underneath the motorhome into a puddle. I have to hand it to him, his rigging worked and the motorhome engine fired right up. Brad was back in the driver's seat, and we headed onward on our journey to Hot Springs, Arkansas.

CHAPTER TEN

When Hunger Strikes …

After another gas stop, we switched driving turns. I was unnerved at having to steer the mammoth around the one-lane mountain roads heading into the Hot Springs area. Dusk was starting to settle, and it was getting more difficult to see in the distance. I drove poking along slowly and probably made several drivers behind me quite angry by my turtle pace. Often a crazy person would swoop around me when they couldn't even see if another car was coming across the hill in the opposite direction.

It was evening when I eventually pulled into the Hot Springs National Park campground. We were down to the bare necessities for food. The campground didn't have shower facilities, only restrooms, and we had no septic and only cold water. I was tired and figured at that point, I would wash Cindy and myself off in the restroom sink. Brad took over backing the mammoth motorhome onto the campsite lot with his mom guiding him in with a lantern.

Brad, Cindy, and I walked to the ranger station to pay. It was unmanned and had a pay machine that would accept credit card or cash payments for the campsite. I paid for the campsite on my credit card and took the receipt. As we walked back to the motorhome, Cindy gazed at the fireflies in the dark with fascination. "Pretty, aren't they, sweetie?" I asked her.

"Uh-huh," she replied while staring and trying to walk with us. She had never seen fireflies before since we don't have them in the Tampa Bay area.

When we arrived back to the motorhome, we agreed we were all getting hungry. Since we still had leftovers from when we went to the sports bar and the steakhouse, Marge and I started foraging through them. I munched down on my half-hamburger from the steakhouse, and Marge and Cindy snacked on the remaining potato skins, broccoli, and chicken wings.

Brad grumbled, "I don't want any of that. I want a big, delicious, hot pepperoni pizza. Someplace around here has got to deliver."

I checked my cellphone and found a pizza delivery in Hot Springs. I entered the address into the GPS. It was only 1.6 miles away. Brad called and asked, "Will you deliver to the Hot Spring National Park Campground?"

The pizza guy replied, "Are you at the KOA Campground?"

"No," Brad answered. "We're at the Hot Springs National Park Campground."

"Our entire city's the national park, so what campground are you in?"

Brad looked at me with a puzzled expression. "It shows the Hot Springs National Park Campground on the sign and on my receipt." I told him.

Brad repeated to him again, "The Hot Springs National Park Campground."

"We need an address."

"Hold on," Brad told him.

I looked on the brochure I had picked up from the ranger station, and the only address it referenced was the Visitors' Center in the historic district of the town. Then I grabbed up the GPS and entered the address of the pizza place from my cellphone.

"Tell him I don't have an address, but I can give him street directions from the pizza place to here."

Brad reiterated what I said. The guy again told him they need an exact address. Brad hung up irritated.

"Have a chicken wing," I said with a mouth full and holding out a drumstick.

"I don't want chicken wings. I want a pizza," he pouted and walked out to the picnic table where Marge was now sitting with a lantern and smoking a cigarette.

"Well, when is the pizza going to get here?" she asked him.

"It's not. They don't know where we are to deliver to us, and I don't have an address for here. Without an exact address, they won't deliver to us. I have a mind to pack up and drive up there."

From the open door, I overheard him and replied, "If we drive off, we'll lose our campsite, especially if someone else pulls into it since we've already paid."

"I'll stay here if you want to go and get you a pizza," Marge offered. "Just leave me the lantern, and I'll be as happy as I can be."

"You're going to sit here in the dark at the picnic table in the woods all by yourself? No way," I said shaking my head.

Brad was all for it. "Just leave her the paid receipt so they won't think that she's just some homeless person that walked up."

I gave Marge the campsite receipt grimacing at the both of them. Brad, Cindy, and I stepped back into the motorhome and drove off leaving the old woman defenseless and sitting at a picnic table with a lantern in the dark, smoking a cigarette and watching fireflies. Boy, did I feel guilty visualizing a large Sasquatch monster picking up my mother in-law and carrying her off like a little ragdoll. But I had to go to help navigate Brad to the pizza place and back.

Brad drove the mammoth off the campsite lot and headed out according to the GPS directions. When we arrived in the small town, the GPS gave me last minute notice of turning left into the pizza delivery parking lot. Brad couldn't maneuver the motorhome into the sharp turn, so he had to drive around the block. He turned right at the first street of opportunity, Hill Street. The street definitely lived up to its name.

Hill Street went straight up almost ninety degrees vertical and dropped down at the same angle on the other side. It was a tight and narrow street. If there was any oncoming traffic, they would not be able to get by the mammoth motorhome. At the top of the peak, it seemed like we pivoted like a seesaw and couldn't see the road below us until we started going straight down. As soon as we started dropping down the hill, everything loose in the motorhome started flying forward toward the front. Toys and books flew across the floor, and I jumped from the passenger chair to the sofa to make sure Cindy was locked tight on the sofa.

"Weee, fun!" Cindy squealed in delight.

"Not fun," I replied crawling beside her onto the sofa. I made sure the seatbelt was secure and slid back over to the passenger seat. Looking out, I saw the sharp turn in the road at the bottom.

"Oh Lord, I hope you can make that turn," I prayed.

Brad made the turn jumping the curb and sending us bouncing in our seats and rattling dishes and cookware. "That was close," he said while turning into the parking lot. He pulled along the backside of a building on the lot and walked to the pizza place while Cindy and I waited inside the motorhome.

He was all smiles when he came back inside carrying his pizza box. "Did you tell them you were the one who called from Hot Springs National Park Campground?" I asked.

"Yeah, I did."

"Oh, then there's probably spit on the pizza."

"I don't care. I'm hungry," he whined and munched happily as he started driving off with a pizza slice in one hand and the steering wheel in the other.

When we pulled back into the campground, Marge was still at the picnic table smoking a cigarette, just like we left her. She helped Brad guide the mammoth back again bay waving the lantern. It was after 9:00 p.m. and pitch dark by the time we got parked and settled again. Brad dug through the outside storage cabinet and found a set of exterior rope lights that were given to us with the motorhome. He plugged them into the exterior outlet and draped the lights around the passenger mirror and over the side entrance door making a glowing sloppy bell curve.

"Yeah, now that really looks redneck," I chuckled while sitting at the picnic table with Marge and Cindy.

"Well at least it's some lighting," he mumbled with a mouth full of pizza. "You'll definitely know which motorhome ours is coming out of the restrooms."

I had to admit, he was right about that. We couldn't be missed, and definitely could not mistake our motorhome for anyone else's. However looking around, there were only three other campers parked in proximity to us. This was obviously a secluded campground, which probably explains why the pizza guy didn't know the location for delivery.

After getting our fill of food and taking splash baths in the restroom sinks, we worked on our sleeping arrangements. There was no way we were going to use the bunk bed. We agreed that Cindy would sleep with Marge on the fold-out couch, and Brad would sleep on the twin bed opposite the one I had been sleeping on.

Cindy grunted and groaned all during the night. I could hear her from the back area where I was lying. Brad woke up asking to switch beds with me, complaining that the mattress was too hard and uncomfortable.

"The mattresses are exactly the same. It wouldn't matter," I told him as I rolled on my side with my back facing him. He grumbled and crawled back over into the other twin bed and finally went to sleep.

In the morning, we all looked like we had a rough night. Marge had taken a muscle relaxer, so she didn't hear Cindy grunting and groaning in her sleep. Marge stretched and moaned saying she felt bruised all over. Cindy must have used her like a kickboxing bag during the night. She could hardly get up and get moving between the muscle relaxer and being kicked all night.

After splashing ourselves awake in the restrooms, we decided to hunt down some breakfast. That was the easy part. I had already seen a fast food restaurant last night while we were on the hunt for pizza. In fact, it was right across the street from the pizza delivery store. I knew there would be no argument from Brad or Cindy when it came to having a fast food breakfast.

The breakfast time crowd had the parking lot packed full and the drive-thru line was wrapped around the building. There was no convenient parking in the lot for the motorhome, but the look in Brad's eyes told me he was going to attempt it.

"Don't even try parking in there!" I demanded. "Look, there's a store right next to it with an empty parking lot. You can park there. Marge and I can walk over and get the food."

"Alright," he said agreeably as he made a hard left-hand turn into the lot. Brad gave us his order of the usual bagel and egg sandwich, and Marge and I marched over to the restaurant on our mission to get breakfast.

As we walked across the vehicles in the parking lot in our daisy-duke shorts, some desperate construction guys were doing cat-calls, yelling, "Shake it! Woohoo!"

Marge and I were so tired we acted oblivious to them and focused on getting some coffee into our bodies. When we returned to the motorhome with the food, Brad asked,

"Did you notice the guys hollering at you two, telling you to shake it?"

I responded, "It must be the mountain-air making those guys hallucinate. Although now, Marge is a hot-looking grandma. She can still shake it." Marge just grimaced while sipping her coffee.

When Brad finished eating his breakfast sandwich, he started up the motorhome and turned it in the direction toward the Historic Hot Springs district. I told him that based on the brochure, there should be parking at the Visitors' Center. He kept on driving past the Visitors' Center, and I noticeably started pouting. "You're not going to stop?" I whined questioning his intentions.

"Yeah, I was going to check out the town, do some sightseeing, and then turn around."

"Oh, okay," I replied, skeptical of his plans.

CHAPTER ELEVEN

Parking 101

Along the narrow street departing from the main historic district, there were several well-maintained older Victorian homes tiered along the hillside. Scalloped molding accented the front porches and steep gabled roofs stretched upwards. Many of the homes had unusual, eye-catching color combinations, such as Pepto-Bismol pink siding with mint green trim, or brick red siding with forest green trim. Further up the mountainside, stately mansions with columnar porches jutted from the hillside overseeing the town.

When it seemed that we had reached more of a regular residential area, Brad directed the motorhome back around and start heading toward the historic spa and shopping district as he said he would. As we drove back into the shopping district, most of the parking lots he drove up to had signs that stated, "No RV's or trailers."

I mentioned to him again that there was parking down at the Visitors' Center. He replied frustrated, "Well, I'll just park right here," as he whipped the motorhome into three parallel parking spots on the side of the street in front of some of the shops in the historic district.

The sound of metal-to-metal grating reverberated through the motorhome. Brad looked out into the driver's side mirror, arched his eyebrows up in a grin, and casually said, "I just ripped the front end grill off of a GMC Yukon."

"Please tell me you're kidding," I begged. I had thought maybe he had hit the light pole on the side of the street. Sure enough, when I lifted the back curtain and looked out, the front end of a white GMC Yukon had its grill just barely hanging on at an angle touching the ground.

"Oh, my God, oh my God, oh my God!" I said frantically as I started scrambling through the bed table drawers for the insurance and registration information. I was praying I had put the black binder containing all the vehicle papers back in one of the drawers. I let out a sigh of relief when I found it in the bottom drawer. I pulled out the registration and insurance papers, ran back to the front, and shoved them at Brad. He was really too calm to suit me. He seemed to be moving in sloth-mode as he picked up his wallet from the console and slid it into his back pocket as I was otherwise frantically running around the motorhome trying to find Cindy's shoes.

While I stuffed Cindy's feet into the pair of shoes, Brad and Marge nonchalantly stepped out of the side door. Cindy and I stepped out after them with me wrestling Cindy to keep her out of the street. I couldn't believe the damage that Brad's parking attempt had done to the motorhome too.

Water was squirting out in force from a broken exterior spout above the back bumper. All our clean water from the interior tank under the twin bed was gushing out onto the street. The exterior electric outlet that we had used for the outside rope lights the night before had been concaved into a deep dent in the motorhome's side. Brad had pulled in too close to the streetlight pole, and it had gashed the side of the motorhome.

A stylish lady, possibly in her early fifties, wearing glasses and an apron, stepped out the ice cream shop near where the Yukon was parked.

"Oh well," she calmly sighed, "I just replaced the driver's side mirror last week. They drive so fast down this road, it was ripped off. That's why it's turned in now," she said pointing her pen toward the driver's side.

"I missed your mirror, and I'm really sorry about hitting your SUV." Brad said apologetically as he gave her the insurance and registration papers. She had walked out with a clipboard and a paper pad and started writing down the insurance information.

She looked at Marge, and I overheard her say, "I wish he would've at least hit the rear bumper. It had a crack in it and needed replacing." Her calm and kindness was a blessing. I was stressing out over the situation, and Cindy's bad behavior was elevating it. She kept attempting to wriggle from my grasp, and the tug-of-war with her was adding to my stress and exhausting me.

As a police officer came up and started writing down the accident information, I walked Cindy over to the display windows of a boutique. Displayed in the window were dinner plates that had painted reproductions of famous artist paintings. A couple of works that I readily recognized were Van Gogh's Starry Night and Monet's Water lilies. I was trying to focus on anything but the carnage happening in front of me.

Cindy absolutely did not want to stand there. She wanted to be with Grandma Marge, who was now standing in the street between the vehicles looking at the Yukon's dilapidated grill. She was adamant to be with Grandma by pulling at my grip, and I had enough of her shenanigans. I picked her up, carried her back into the motorhome, and plopped her on the couch. "Sit and don't move," I threatened while locking the motorhome door with us in it.

Cindy started crying as I walked to the back of the motorhome and looked out the back window. Another lady had stepped out of the ice cream shop and was talking to Marge. Brad had his toolbox out and was working on removing the Yukon's grill so the owner could at least drive it home. Marge left the other woman's side and started walking toward the motorhome. I went back and unlocked the side door.

Marge was snickering as she stepped inside. "You're not going to believe the story the other lady told me," she giggled. "She said her and her husband had a camper, and while they were driving down the interstate, the sewage line had broken loose. It sprayed cars for a couple of miles down the road until they figured out what had happened. Brad and I just looked at her and said 'Well, at least that hasn't happened to us.' We didn't tell her that we had lost the entire septic system."

Marge had really gotten tickled over the whole ordeal. "She offered the baby some chocolate ice cream, if you want to take her into the shop."

I looked over at Cindy, who was now softly sniffling. "Would you like to go get some ice cream?"

"Uh-huh," she responded quietly.

"Come on. Let's go get you some," I said with a sigh.

As we stepped back out of the motorhome, Marge said, "Brad couldn't have hit the car of a nicer person. Even the police officer has been really nice through this. Most of them I've met are usually jerks. He couldn't have been a more of a pleasant cop." I guess she thought saying this would help console my stress.

When we approached where Brad was standing, he was asking the police officer if we could stay parked in the spot and visit the shops, especially since the motorhome was already parked there, and he had done enough damage with this parking attempt.

"Certainly, but there's a two-hour time limit," the officer replied. "A meter person will come by and mark your tires and then come back around and ticket it if it hasn't been moved after the second set of marks."

I overheard Brad thanking him as Marge, Cindy and I were walking into the ice cream shop. The Yukon lady gave Cindy a small cup of chocolate ice cream, and I bought a couple of flavored rock candy sticks to take home to Kelly. The nice lady looked at me and asked "Would you like a cup of coffee, honey? You look a little frazzled."

"No thank you, ma'am. I really appreciate it, but the last thing I need right now is caffeine. I'm jittery enough as is."

Brad walked into the fudge shop and sat for a couple a minutes. He then stood up and paced uncomfortably through the ice cream shop while Cindy took her time slurping on the ice cream. He was feeling guilty about the damage he had caused to the kind lady's vehicle, and it showed by his excessive pacing.

"Can you get Cindy to hurry up? I really don't want to stay in here," he whispered to me.

"She'll be done soon. She fills up quick. Just wait," I replied.

A few minutes later, Cindy said, "I full" and handed me her empty ice cream cup.

We again thanked the lady for the ice cream and her patience and left the ice cream shop. Walking down the shopping district, we came to a toy store. Cindy was excited to go inside. She made a bee-line straight to the wooden train railway in the middle of the floor.

As she started playing with the trains, an elderly gentleman walked up and started talking to Brad and Marge. He was the store owner and informed them that everything in the store was for children's hands-on imaginative play, so he did not carry any electronic games. He asked Brad where we were from.

Brad replied, "Florida. We're heading to Oklahoma to take my mom back home."

"You're the ones in the camper?" the gentleman asked smiling.

Brad blushed and answered, "Yeah, we just had a little fender bender."

"I saw that," said the store owner with a smile on his face.

I piped up, "Brad, he obviously knows it was you. You're wearing a bright neon green t-shirt. You can't be missed."

Sure enough, Brad's bright green t-shirt could not be overlooked. While he had worked on removing the grill from the Yukon, many of the shop owners peeped out of their stores to see what had happened. He stood out like a neon billboard.

"Things happen like that around here. We frequently have accidents out front, but it's usually because someone is speeding down the street," replied the store owner.

He continued showing Brad and Marge around the store. They eventually walked up to the wooden train set where I was standing, and Cindy was busily playing. Cindy was so fascinated with the train set and the gentleman was so kind, we ended up buying a starter train kit for her.

After we left the store, we continued walking down the strip. We entered a novelty store that had several tourist souvenirs for Hot Springs, custom earthware jewelry, and hippie merchandise such as mood rings and tie-dyed clothing. As I was looking at the Himalayan salt lamps, I overheard the guy working the register say, "Hey, it's the killer RV dude!"

I glanced over at Brad and by the look on his face, I thought he was going to die of embarrassment. "Yeah, that's me. You may want to stay off the street while I'm here," Brad replied forcing a grin.

As I walked past Brad I said in a whisper, "It's the shirt. You can't miss it. By the way, what happened to 'make sure you swing the rear-end around, you got to watch for that extra thirty-three feet'?" I antagonized him. "Looks like someone didn't follow their own driving directions."

Brad just grunted and walked away from me annoyed. I had to get his goat from all the backseat driving and preaching he had given me. Sometimes it pays to follow the instructions given to others.

After we had perused the stores on the one side of the district, we crossed the street where the historical bathhouses were located. I felt disappointed because I had figured that the bathhouses in Hot Springs would be more like open public bathing pools. Instead, it proved to be more for the upscale spa goers, and those who had advance reservations. We eventually went into the Fordyce Bathhouse that the National Park Service had converted into a visitor center and small museum. While there, we watched a short video clip on the history of Hot Springs.

Upon leaving the visitor center, Cindy picked out a bright orange emergency whistle with a Hot Springs logo as a souvenir. She enjoyed blowing it loud and long as we walked along the sidewalk. I knew she was going to enjoy torturing us in the motorhome.

As we crossed the street and headed back toward the motorhome, the meter maid pranced happily along marking the tires of vehicles parked along the side street. She stood alongside the motorhome, bent over, and marked the tires with a yellow crayon as we walked up. We figured that was our cue to leave.

Brad used extra caution and pulled carefully out of the parking spaces, looking back and making sure no cars were flying down the street beside us. We were heading to our final destination of Johnson County, Oklahoma. I was actually at the point of having enough of sightseeing and traveling. I was ready to stay put in one location for a few days.

We travelled along the curving roads of Arkansas to highway US-70 west into Oklahoma. Marge was able help Brad with navigation while Cindy and I took afternoon naps on the back beds. Cindy and I woke up when Brad started bouncing us along the dirt roads heading up toward Marge's house.

CHAPTER TWELVE

The Rooster has Landed

Marge's property represents what some people would call the "boonies." She lives on ninety acres of woods and pasture land in which coyotes, wild boar, bobcats, and deer roam wild. Marge's neighbors are distant from each with exception to Brad's brother, John, his wife Tracy, and kids. They live approximately a quarter mile down the road from Marge. The only access to the property from the main road is over eight miles of red clay and rock roads.

When we eventually arrived at Marge's house and stepped out of the motorhome, it was like we had driven into Hell. It was HOT! The Midwest had been experiencing triple digit heat this summer, and it had to be at least 110 degrees outside. I'm always complaining that I'm cold, so when I'm saying someplace is hot, it's HOT. I actually couldn't wait to get back into air conditioning.

Brad and I unloaded the remaining perishables from the motorhome. Since Marge did not have an outside electric outlet for us to plug into, we had to remove anything that would go bad when the motorhome started heating up from the outside temperatures. Eventually, we had everything pulled out and were finally able to relax.

We spent a couple of days at Marge's house, enjoying the peace and quiet of the countryside. The house is a small, cozy version of a farmhouse and probably no bigger than 600 square feet in size. The house has been in Marge's family for more than eighty years and was built by her father before she was born. Over the years, she has added modern facets and conveniences, such as gray-colored vinyl exterior siding, a storm door, wall unit air-conditioning, insulated windows, satellite television and internet, and an exterior utility room addition.

Marge keeps herself busy with caring for her four horses, chickens, and her old beagle dog, Bailey. There's a large fishing pond in the wooded area, and Brad and his brother frequently walked down to see if they could catch any of the bass from the shallows.

Toward the evening when the temperature started cooling off, I stretched out on Marge's outside rocking bench to relax. I could hear the peaceful mooing of neighboring cows in the distance. While lying there, I heard a clucking sound behind the rocker and didn't think much of it. Next thing I knew, Marge's rooster jumped up on the top rail of the bench, unexpectedly startling me and almost making me flip myself off the bench.

"Dammit!" I yelled, "You don't have to be right on top of me bird … geez." The bird just stood there, cocked his head to one side and stared at down at me.

I pushed the bench rocker with my foot in an attempt to shake the bird from his perch. Since the rooster wouldn't budge off the bench, I stood up and started to walk toward the back porch of house. As I walked, I heard flapping. I looked back, and sure enough, the rooster was stalking me!

I went inside the house and told Marge, "I think your rooster is infatuated with me."

"Oh yeah, Roo likes blondes. He probably thinks you're me and that you have food," Marge replied.

"Great," I thought, "I have a hungry lovesick rooster after me."

After a late dinner, we set off for bed. For sleeping arrangements, Brad and I slept in the full size bed in Marge's spare bedroom, and Cindy slept with Marge in her queen bed. The next morning at the crack of dawn, Brad and I were awakened by Roo crowing right by the bedroom window. The rooster had figured out where I was. Brad said, "Your boyfriend is looking for you."

"My boyfriend is going to come for dinner if he's not careful, and he's going to be the main course," I groaned crawling out of bed and stretching my stiff back.

I walked into the kitchen and started making some much needed coffee. Marge came in and said cheerfully, "Well you're up bright and early."

"No thanks to your rooster," I grunted. "He's going to become dinner if he keeps it up."

"Awww, don't hurt my Roo-Roo," Marge replied sweetly. "He likes you."

Sure enough, the rooster followed me all during the day when I was in Marge's fenced-in yard area surrounding the house. The only time he did not stalk me was when I would walk with Brad and Cindy to the pond for fishing or down to John's house to visit the family. I guess old Roo knew not to venture outside of Marge's fence line because he could become a coyote's juicy dinner. He seemed to enjoy being a nuisance and woke us up at the crack of dawn again the next morning.

CHAPTER THIRTEEN

The Haunted

Since the motorhome had its problem issues going to Marge's from Florida, Brad and I decided to leave Friday morning so we would have plenty of time to get home just in case the motorhome decided to act up again. I needed to be back in time for work again on Monday.

We packed the motorhome up with some basic food necessities such as milk, juice, and other edibles and hugged and kissed my wonderful little mother in-law goodbye. Brad took over the initial driving duties, and we headed out in the direction back east toward Hot Springs, Arkansas.

As we headed out onto the main road, I asked Brad sarcastically if he would like to stop in Hot Springs and visit the ice cream shop again on our way out. He glared at me and said "No frigging way am I ever going back there!"

Our trip out was relatively peaceful with no incidents as we drove along toward Hot Springs. It was how a traveling trip should be. Cindy played with her new train set on the floor. Brad and I enjoyed chatting about our trip and the family. The weather was beautiful and not a cloud in the sky.

By late afternoon, we had reached the renowned KOA Campground in Hot Springs and decided to stay there so Cindy could play in the swimming pool. The campground cashier assigned us a site by the bathhouse, and Brad backed the motorhome into it.

Once we settled into the campsite, the three of us walked down to the campground pool and went swimming. Cindy bounced around in the shallow end and played with another little girl her age. Brad left before Cindy and me in order to cook bratwurst on the grill for dinner. When I had enough of being water-logged, I dragged a tired, kicking and screaming Cindy from the pool away from her new playmate. No wonder why Brad volunteered to be the one to cook dinner. He must have known that Cindy would have been a challenge to remove from the pool.

After eating dinner and changing into some dry clothes, we joined the campground festivities that were provided. Around dusk, the campground held a candy treasure hunt for the kids in the playground area. Cindy had fun seeking out the candy and putting it in the plastic grocery bag provided by the campground. She would run as fast as her chubby little legs would carry her to get the candy pieces. Frequently an older kid would beat her to the piece, and she would sit on the ground pouting until Brad picked her up and took her to another piece. At times, she definitely acted like a spoiled only child.

After the candy hunt, we returned to the motorhome to collect the bathroom toiletries, clean clothes, and headed to the bathrooms. The bathrooms were very clean and spacious. Cindy took a warm shower with me and enjoyed playing and giggling in the bubbles from the shampoo.

When we returned to the motorhome, I read Cindy the Disney story book, Snow White and the Seven Dwarfs. She rested on the twin bed across from me, playing with her Spongebob pillow as she listened. Brad had folded out the sofa couch and was already asleep and snoring deeply.

In the morning, we went to a fast food joint, grabbed our usual breakfast items to-go, and then ventured back out on the road. I was praying for another peaceful day on the road just as the previous day had been. I figured maybe it was Marge's luck that was jinxing the trip. There's never a dull moment when she's around.

In order to shorten the drive time home, I focused navigating our route southward toward interstate 10 which would take us directly east to Florida. This was a mistake I would soon regret.

Before we had left Oklahoma, the weather newscast had mentioned a tropical storm brewing in the Gulf of Mexico. The interstate 10 route would take us through sections in Mississippi and Louisiana that were below sea-level. The extensive rains would make travel in some of these southeastern areas difficult due to flooding. I didn't even think about this issue. I just wanted to get home the fastest way possible per the GPS navigation, which was the interstate 10 route.

The weather had remained pretty clear as we drove southeastward through Arkansas. I relaxed in the passenger chair navigating the route for Brad, and Cindy played with her trains behind me and snacked on her candy from the campground. Eventually, some of the detour routes that I directed Brad to drive were extremely bumpy. As Brad hit a hard bump in the road with the motorhome, I felt extreme pain in my head and everything went black on me. I saw stars like you see in cartoon shows. The clasps on both ends of the bunk bed had broken simultaneously causing the bed to slam down on top of both of our heads.

Brad started yelling, "Get it up, get it up, so I can drive!"

Still stunned from the smack on the head, I staggered to stand up and pushed upwards on the bunk bed with all my strength. I could hardly budge the bed upwards. Brad quickly pulled to the side of the road and said, "That's it! I'm going to fix it where it'll never come down!"

I thought, "Uh oh," as we pushed it up together and securely latched it again. As luck would have it, we had driven into a small town with a roadside Mom and Pop hardware shop. Brad pulled into the side of the parking lot, and the three of us climbed out and went inside.

Brad bought two steel plates about four inches long and three inches high with multiple holes cut out in them. He also purchased several sheet metal screws. He asked the man at the register if they had a drill he could borrow.

"No sir, I don't but you can rent one from the equipment shop down the street," he replied.

Brad told him thanks, and we back out to our monstrosity. He said, "I'm doing it the old-fashioned way," and asked me to help hold the bunk closed tight. I again strained to push it upwards and hold it in place, and he started hand-tightening the screws into the steel plates on both sides of the bunk.

He complained that his hands were sore after fastening all the screws, but it definitely looked like the bunk would finally be fixed from dropping down. Of course, now the bed couldn't be used anymore, but at least it wouldn't be dropping on our heads.

Through the rest of the afternoon, the ride was relaxing with us only making a couple of stops for snacks and gas and taking turns driving. The peacefulness was short lived when we arrived in Mississippi. Brad was driving and heading right into the rains and strong winds from the tropical storm. The gusts beat and swayed the motorhome, and the downpour made it difficult for us to see out the windshield even with the wipers sweeping the rain away.

Suddenly, both wipers stopped vertical on the windshield. Brad commented, "Now what!" and started beating on the dash. "This motorhome has to be haunted. Someone must have died in here for all this to be happening."

I knew he was upset, but I started giggling under the stress. "It's not haunted. It's the neon green shirt. It's bad luck, and you have it on again."

Sure enough, Brad had the same bright neon green shirt on that he had worn when he hit the Yukon in Hot Springs. As soon as I said that, Brad ripped off the shirt, rolled down the driver side window, and shoved the shirt out into the rain. The wipers immediately started working again. We just stared at each other, unbelieving what just had occurred, and then burst out in laughter.

"Told you so!" I bellowed.

Since the winds and rain kept a constant beating on us, and it was getting toward evening, we decided to find a campground. From what I could tell from the GPS and the road map, we were close to a small Mississippi state park. When we arrived at the ranger station, we found out that what seemed to be a small state park on the map was actually an upscale campground with a lake and golf course. I told Brad we would have to visit this state park again when the weather was more tolerable.

As Cindy and I took I shower at the bath house, Brad setup the motorhome and made us some sandwiches for dinner. Since it was muggy and steamy outside from the rain, Brad had the air conditioner running full-force inside the motorhome. He loves it cold when he sleeps. I'd rather be comfortably warm. Snuggled under the blankets, I fell into a deep, comfortable sleep. Later, I was rudely awakened by the smell of something electrical burning and a feeling of being sweaty and sticky. I heard Brad cussing about the air conditioner. It was on the blitz and was absolutely fried by the wretched smell of it.

Brad went outside in the sprinkling rain and climbed on top of the motorhome to see what he could do to get the air conditioning unit working again. I heard him stomping around on the rooftop and prayed he wouldn't find a soft spot and accidently fall through. That would be all we would need right now. His attempt at getting the air conditioner working was futile. It wasn't going to happen. The motorhome was becoming warm and muggy from the rain and humidity outside.

Brad eventually gave up and climbed down from the top of the motorhome. I heard him digging around the outside storage compartment and then he walked back into the motorhome. He was drenched from being rained on and had carried in a box fan from the outside storage compartment. He set the fan up on the front console to blow back into the sleeping area for some kind of air circulation inside.

CHAPTER FOURTEEN

Here comes the rain again …

After a muggy night of sleep, we took showers again in the morning at the restroom facilities. As Brad drove out of the campground, he cussed and fussed about the air conditioner going out. I reminded him that at least the dash air still worked to keep us cool while driving. The weather was still misting rain as we left Percy Quin and headed back southward onto interstate 55. Brad's grumbling stomach finally got the best of him, and we stopped at another fast food restaurant for a quick breakfast.

Eventually, we connected to interstate 12 in Louisiana and started heading east toward Florida. The roads were flooded in areas making traffic crawl to a snail's pace, and the rain beat the motorhome on all sides causing it to sway along the roadway. The tropical storm had caused considerable flooding in the Louisiana and southern Alabama areas. It was a nerve-racking drive.

Brad became exhausted from maneuvering the motorhome and asked if I could drive. I knew it would be a white-knuckle ride through the storm, but I just wanted to get home at that point.

"Yeah, I guess I better if I want to get home," I replied.

Brad pulled off at a rest area, and I took over the driver's seat. He walked to the back bed and played with Cindy and her Lego blocks for a little bit. Eventually, they were both sound asleep taking naps.

I drove in silence and through the torrid rain in Alabama. When I arrived in Mobile, Brad had woken back up and sat in the passenger seat. The rain was beating down hard. A lighted interstate sign directed traffic to take the I-10 bridge because the George Wallace tunnel was under water. I looked at the upcoming bridge with apprehension and thought, "Oh, dear Lord, please help us through this!"

The bridge expanded high over the bay, and the winds and rain pushed hard against motorhome causing me to drive at a cautiously slow pace. As we approached the uppermost part of the bridge, the wipers stopped dead again in a vertical position along the windshields. I thought to myself, "You got to be kidding me. Please, please start back working." As if the wipers read my thoughts, they started back swiping back and forth as I drove along on the downside of the bridge.

My hands were aching and sweaty from gripping the steering wheel too tight. As I turned off the bridge and started toward Battleship Parkway, I couldn't believe my eyes. The ramp going onto Battleship Parkway was flooded with waves lapping against the roadway. We had nowhere else to go but to plow through the floodwaters on the ramp. I steered the motorhome onto the ramp and prayed we wouldn't stall or be swept away into the gulf. The traffic was crawling, and the only visible features through the down-pouring rain were red taillights of braking vehicles ahead.

Brad looked at me and said, "You really are determined to get home aren't you."

"Heck yeah!" I replied, deeply focused on my driving. "I've had enough traveling for now. I want to be at home in my own bed."

Once we cleared the parkway and crossed into Florida, it was smooth driving along the interstate. The rains finally eased up, and we decided to stop in Pensacola at a Chinese restaurant for something to eat. After eating, I told Brad I was okay to continue driving. He headed to the back beds and took another nap while Cindy entertained herself with her toys. As he napped, I floored the motorhome to get us home. A short time later, he was again standing behind my seat.

"Man, there's a lot of wind noise back there. How fast are you going, Leadfoot?" he asked glancing over my shoulder at the speedometer.

Sometimes, I had it floored going eighty-five miles an hour. "I've been going over seventy," I replied sheepishly.

"Getting a little confident in your driving, aren't ya?" he smirked.

"I just want to get home," I replied anxiously.

It was getting dark as we arrived in the city of Gainesville. Traffic became tighter on all sides, so I had to slow my speed down. I looked in the rear-view mirror, and an idiot driver was right on my tail-end. He started flashing his lights at me to go faster or move over. I had vehicles on both sides of me and in front of me. There was nowhere to go and no way to go faster. I told Brad, "Look at this idiot behind me."

Brad said, "Not a problem. I'll take of him." He walked toward the back of the motorhome and then came back grinning.

"Did he back off?" Brad asked.

"Yeah, it looks like he did. What did you do?" I asked curiously just knowing he had been up to mischief.

"I poured some of the blue septic cleaner down the toilet. I'm sure he got a windshield full."

"Great. We're going to get shot if he's a nutcase. Oh boy!"

Instead the idiot took advantage of a clear spot and sped by us when provided an opportunity. The rest of the ride home was thankfully uneventful. When I pulled into our driveway, it was already after midnight. My cousin, Frankie, who was house-sitting, helped us unload a very sleepy Cindy. Brad parked what we nicknamed "the rolling brown turd" in the back yard.

Later that month, I advertised the motorhome online for five thousand dollars. We figured the lost septic tank and air conditioning would at least cost one thousand dollars. We were also ready to negotiate to a lower price since we knew what escapades the motorhome had endured from our travel.

An older lady contacted Brad informing him of her interest. Brad provided her with the honest disclosure of all the mishaps that occurred during the summer and the missing septic tank. She showed no apprehension in making the purchase and offered forty-five hundred. In fact, she said her intention was to park it on her property for her relatives to stay in when they visited. She planned to run the sewage line directly to her home septic system. It was a match made in heaven for her.

Although we lost money on the motorhome and skimped on the purchase price, the memorable summer vacation and unique experiences made every penny pinched worth it. However, it may be awhile before I purchase another used motorhome. Cheap hotels or even a new motorhome are possibilities in my future vacation plans.

ABOUT THE AUTHOR

M.L. Roberts is an accounting undergraduate of the University of Tampa and has an established career as a professional accounting director. She writes about her family adventures as a hobby. She currently lives in Riverview, Florida, with her husband and youngest of three children.

ABOUT THE BOOK

When the spirit for adventure strikes, a bargain buy on a motorhome, spontaneous travel plans, and a quirky mother-in-law make for an unforgettable and extremely eventful summer vacation for the Roberts family. Follow the comical adventure in the used motorhome as the family travels from their Tampa Bay residence to the blue waters of the Florida Keys for their maiden voyage and initial camping experience in the motorhome. Enjoy the hilarious escapades of the family as they set out for a cross-country trip to the hot, dry flatlands of the Midwest and face the challenges of storm-soaked Southern states in what is expected to be the comforts of home on wheels. Use the whacky family experiences as lessons learned for purchasing a used motorhome and a as guide for what to look for in such a bargain buy.

Printed in the United States
By Bookmasters